Volume

Cups (US)	US fl. oz / pints	Metric
1 tsp		5 ml
1 tbsp	½ fl. oz	15 ml
	⅔ fl. oz	20 ml
2 tbsp	1 fl. oz	30 ml
¼ cup	2 fl. oz	60 ml
⅓ cup	2 ¾ fl. oz	80 ml
	3 fl. oz	90 ml
½ cup	¼ pint	120 ml
	5 fl. oz	150 ml
⅔ cup	5 ½ fl. oz	160 ml
¾ cup	6 fl. oz	180 ml
	6 ¾ fl. oz	200 ml
1 cup	½ pint	240 ml
1 ¼ cups	10 fl. oz	300 ml
1 ½ cups	12 fl. oz	355 ml
1 ¾ cups	14 fl. oz	415 ml
2 cups	1 pint	475 ml
2 ½ cups	1 ¼ pints	590 ml
3 cups	1 ½ pints	710 ml
3 ½ cups	1 ¾ pints	830 ml
4 cups	2 pints	950 ml

Metric	Imperial	Cups (UK)
5 ml		1 tsp
15 ml	½ fl. oz	1 tbsp
20 ml	⅔ fl. oz	1 Aus tbsp
30 ml	1 fl. oz	2 tbsp
60 ml	2 fl. oz	¼ cup
80 ml	2 ¾ fl. oz	⅓ cup
85 ml	3 fl. oz	
120 ml	4 ¼ fl. oz	½ cup
150 ml	¼ pint	
160 ml	5 ⅔ fl. oz	⅔ cup
180 ml	6 ⅓ fl. oz	¾ cup
200 ml	7 fl. oz	
240 ml	8 ½ fl. oz	1 cup
300 ml	10 ½ fl. oz	1 ¼ cups
360 ml	12 ⅔ fl. oz	1 ½ cups
420 ml	¾ pint	1 ¾ cups
480 ml	17 fl. oz	2 cups
600 ml	1 pint	2 ½ cups
720 ml	1 ¼ pints	3 cups
840 ml	1 ½ pints	3 ½ cups
960 ml		4 cups

Butter

Spoons	Sticks	Cups	Imperial	Metric
1 tbsp				
2 tbsp	¼ stick		1 oz	28 g
3 tbsp				
4 tbsp	½ stick	¼ cup	2 oz	57 g
5 tbsp		⅓ cup		
6 tbsp	¾ stick		3 oz	85 g
7 tbsp				
8 tbsp	1 stick	½ cup	4 oz	113 g

The great fairy bake off

make
believe
ideas

Welcome to
the great fairy bake off

Camilla the Cupcake Fairy and her friends love to bake cakes and treats for each other. Once a year they get together for the biggest competition in Fairyland – the great fairy bake off!

Inside this special book you will find each fairy's favourite recipes. All the recipes will be entered into the bake off – which one do you think will win first prize?

Camilla the Cupcake Fairy

Camilla is Fairyland's youngest fairy.
She is five years old and has a special
wand that makes toppings for cupcakes.
Her best friends are Maya and Molly.

Camilla

Molly

Maya

Daisy

Daisy the Doughnut Fairy

Daisy lives with her sisters, Dee and
Dolly, in a lighthouse made of doughnuts!
They love to bake doughnuts but have
some other special recipes
they'd love to share!

Dolly

Dee

Lola the Lollipop Fairy

Lola and her sisters, Lulu and Linda, star in a famous circus show. They think cakes taste best when you eat them off sticks – just like lollipops!

Lola

Linda

Lulu

Izzy

Mo

Mia

Izzy the Ice-cream Fairy

Izzy and her special friends, Mo and Mia, live on a beautiful beach next to a magical ice-cream well! Izzy's recipes are perfect for hot, sunny days.

Annie the Apple Pie Fairy

Annie has her own TV show and she is a Fairyland family favourite. She loves baking pies most of all. Her best friends are Pip and Cora.

Annie

Cora

Pip

Katie the Candy Cane Fairy

Katie is a singer who performs in a magical Christmas show with her friends, Crystal and Glo. They love anything with stripes – especially candy canes! Katie's bakes make delicious Christmas treats.

Katie

Glo

Crystal

Taking care

Follow Camilla's easy kitchen rules and you will make sure that baking time is always magical!

Get ready!

♥ Wash and dry your hands before you do anything. Nobody wants your germs!

♥ If you have long hair like Katie the Candy Cane Fairy, tie it back so it doesn't fall in your food!

♥ Put on an apron to keep your clothes nice and clean.

Get organised!

♥ Clear plenty of space to work.

♥ Find all the equipment you need and put it all together in one place.

♥ Measure out all the ingredients you need and put them to one side.*

* Please note: throughout this book, 1 international tbsp = 15 ml / ½ fl. oz. If you live in Australia, please use the ml and fl. oz measurements where given to avoid confusion.

Get going!

♥ Follow the recipe carefully.

♥ Knives can be dangerous. Always ask an adult to help with cutting and slicing.

♥ Never touch anything electrical with wet hands.

♥ Always keep pan handles turned to the side so they cannot be knocked over as you walk past.

♥ When using the oven or handling anything hot, always wear oven gloves or use a pot holder, and ask an adult to help you.

Contents

What you need

Here are all the things Camilla and her friends use to make perfect cakes and treats!

measuring cups

measuring spoons

scales

whisk

hand whisk

wooden spoon

palette knife

sharp knife

knife

fork

pastry brush

chopping board

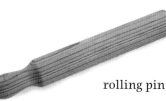
rolling pin

piping bag

flour duster

sieve

cupcake tray

baking tray

square baking tray

"Decorate with fresh strawberries and white chocolate curls."

15

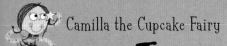

Chocolate delights

Preheat the oven to 180°C / 160°C fan / gas mark 4 and put the cupcake cases in the cupcake tray.

Makes 12

You will need

cupcake tray
12 cupcake cases
scales / measuring cups
measuring spoons
large bowl
whisk
sieve
wooden spoon
teaspoon
wire rack
medium bowl

1 batch / 600 g / 1 lb 5 oz cupcake mixture (see p12)

♥

3 tbsp / 20 g / ¾ oz cocoa powder

♥

1 batch / 400 g / 14 oz chocolate butter icing (see p13)

♥

100 g / 3 ½ oz / ½ cup chocolate buttons

♥

200 g / 7 oz / 4 cups mini marshmallows

♥

1 tbsp icing sugar

16

Making breadcrumbs

1. Wash your hands with cold water and dry them thoroughly.

2. Sieve flour into a bowl.

3. Cut butter into small cubes and add it to the bowl.

4. Using your fingertips, rub the butter into the flour until no large lumps of butter remain and the mix looks like breadcrumbs.

Rolling out

1. Make sure your surface is clean and dry. Sieve flour (for dough and pastry) or icing sugar (for icing) lightly onto the surface and rub over the rolling pin to prevent sticking.

2. Roll dough, pastry or icing into a ball shape. If the dough mixture falls apart, add a few drops of water to stick it together.

3. Place the ball on the floured surface and roll out with the rolling pin. Keep rolling the dough, pastry or icing until it is about 3 mm (¼ in) thick.

4. Cut out shapes with a cookie cutter. When you cannot cut out any more, gather the scraps into a ball and repeat steps 2 and 3. Use a palette knife to help you lift up the cut-out shapes if they are sticking.

Preparing fruit

1. Wash the fruit thoroughly under the tap.

2. Cut off any stalks – for strawberries, run a knife around the stalk to cut out a little of the core, and for apples, carefully peel the skin with a sharp knife.

3. Cut into roughly 5 mm (¼ in) cubes with a sharp knife.

Mashed: Put the chunks in a bowl and mash with a fork.

Puréed: Push the mashed mixture through a large sieve.

Melting chocolate

1. Break the chocolate into small chunks and put in a microwave-safe bowl.

2. Microwave the chocolate for 60 seconds, then take it out and stir it with a spoon.

3. If the chocolate has not fully melted, put it back in the microwave for another 10 seconds. Keep doing this until you can stir out any remaining lumps.

Warning: Do not overcook as this will burn the chocolate!

Fairy cupcakes

Preheat the oven to 180°C / 160°C fan / gas mark 4 and put the cupcake cases in the cupcake tray.

Makes **12** **You will need**

cupcake tray
12 cupcake cases
scales / measuring cups
large bowl
whisk
sieve
wooden spoon
teaspoon
wire rack

3 medium eggs
♥
150 g / 5 ⅓ oz / 1 ⅓ cups
self-raising flour
♥
150 g / 5 ⅓ oz / ⅔ cup
unsalted butter
♥
150 g / 5 ⅓ oz / ¾ cup
caster sugar

1 Beat the eggs in a bowl.

2 Sieve the flour into the bowl, add the butter and sugar and mix for about 2 minutes until it is creamy.

3 Use a teaspoon to put a little mixture into each cupcake case so it is about ¾ full. Bake the cakes in the oven for about 15 minutes until they are golden brown.

"Cool the cakes on a wire rack."

1

Make the cupcake mixture in a bowl, then add the cocoa and mix well.

2

Spoon the mixture into the cupcake cases, bake for about 15 minutes, then cool on a wire rack.

3

Ice the cakes with chocolate butter icing, chocolate buttons and mini marshmallows.

"Dust the finished cakes with icing sugar."

Fairy flutter cakes

Preheat the oven to 180°C / 160°C fan / gas mark 4 and put the cupcake cases in the cupcake tray.

Makes **12**

You will need

cupcake tray

12 cupcake cases

scales / measuring cups

measuring spoons

large bowl

whisk

sieve

wooden spoon

teaspoon

wire rack

knife

medium bowl

1 batch / 600 g / 1 lb 5 oz cupcake mixture (see p12)

♥

100 ml / 3 ½ fl. oz / ½ cup honey

♥

1 batch / 400 g / 14 oz butter icing (see p13)

♥

2 tbsp pink sprinkles

♥

1 tbsp icing sugar

1 Make the cupcake mixture in a bowl.

2 Stir 3 ½ tsp honey into the mixture.

3 Spoon the mixture into the cases, bake for about 15 minutes until golden brown, then cool on a wire rack.

4 Cut out a shallow dip in the centre of a cake, cut the removed piece in half and leave it to one side.

5 Put 1 tsp honey into the dip, then put 2 tsp butter icing on top of the honey and spread it over the cake.

6 Put the cut-out pieces back on top of the cake, sticking out like fairy wings, and add some sprinkles.

"Drizzle honey over your cakes and dust them with icing sugar."

19

Giant cupcake

Preheat the oven to 180°C / 160°C fan / gas mark 4 and grease the tin with butter.

Serves 16

You will need

giant cupcake tin*

scales / measuring cups

measuring spoons

large bowl

sieve

whisk

wooden spoon

wire rack

medium bowl

piping bag

*Alternatively use 3 cake tins (see Treasure island p30).

---

1 tbsp unsalted butter

♥

400 g / 14 oz / 3 ½ cups self-raising flour

♥

8 medium eggs (lightly beaten)

♥

400 g / 14 oz / 1 ¾ cups unsalted butter

♥

400 g / 14 oz / 2 cups caster sugar

♥

2 drops vanilla extract

♥

2 batches / 800 g / 1 lb 12 oz butter icing (see p13)

♥

200 g / 7 oz / 1 cup sprinkles / sweets

1. Sieve the flour into a bowl, add the eggs, butter, sugar and vanilla extract and mix for about 2 minutes until it is creamy.

2. Put the mixture into the tin and bake for 20 minutes until golden brown, then cool on a wire rack.

3. Put the cake together, then cover it with piped icing.

"Decorate with your choice of sweets."

Rockin' rock cakes

Makes 6

You will need

- baking tray
- baking paper
- scales / measuring cups
- large bowl
- wooden spoon
- tablespoon
- wire rack

Preheat the oven to 190°C / 170°C fan / gas mark 5 and grease the tray with butter or line with baking paper.

85 g / 3 oz / ¾ cup self-raising flour

♥

50 g / 1 ¾ oz / ¼ cup unsalted butter

♥

1 small egg

♥

45 g / 1 ½ oz / ¼ cup caster sugar

♥

35 g / 1 ¼ oz / ¼ cup raisins

♥

35 g / 1 ¼ oz / ¼ cup chopped glacé cherries

♥

35 g / 1 ¼ oz / ¼ cup chocolate chips

1 Mix the flour and butter until it has the consistency of breadcrumbs.

2 Stir in the egg, sugar, raisins, cherries and chocolate chips.

3 Put large spoonfuls of the mix onto the tray. Don't smooth them out, as you want them to look like rocks. Bake for 15–20 minutes until they are golden brown.

"Cool the cakes on a wire rack."

Daisy the Doughnut Fairy

Doughnut dinghies

Preheat the oven to
200°C / 180°C fan /
gas mark 6 and grease
the tin with butter.

Makes 10

You will need

doughnut baking tin

scales / measuring cups

measuring spoons

large bowl

sieve

wooden spoon

teaspoon

wire rack

microwave-safe bowl

spoon

---

2 tsp unsalted butter

♥

150 g / 5 ⅓ oz / 1 ⅓ cups
plain flour

♥

1 tsp baking powder

♥

¼ tsp salt

♥

2 medium eggs

♥

2 tbsp / 30 ml / 1 fl. oz
sunflower oil

♥

100 g / 3 ½ oz / ½ cup
caster sugar

♥

200 ml / 7 fl. oz / 1 cup
buttermilk

♥

100 g / 3 ½ oz / ⅔ cup
raspberries

♥

100 g / 3 ½ oz / ½ cup
white cooking chocolate

1 Sieve the flour, baking powder and salt into a bowl.

2 Add the eggs, oil, sugar and buttermilk and mix until smooth.

3 Stir in the raspberries.

4 Spoon the mix into the tin, bake for 15–20 minutes until golden brown, then cool on a wire rack.

5 Melt the chocolate, then drizzle over the doughnuts and leave to dry.

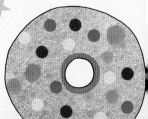

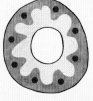

24

"A delicious seaside snack!"

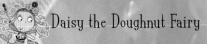

Sparkly starfish

Preheat the oven to
190°C / 170°C fan /
gas mark 5 and line
the baking tray with
baking paper.

Makes
8

You will need

baking tray
baking paper
scales / measuring cups
measuring spoons
large bowl
wooden spoon
rolling pin
star-shaped cookie cutter
wire rack
knife
microwave-safe bowl
spoon

150 g / 5 ⅓ oz / 1 ⅓ cups
plain flour
♥
100 g / 3 ½ oz / 7 tbsp
unsalted butter
♥
50 g / 1 ¾ oz / ¼ cup
caster sugar
♥
500 g / 1 lb
white fondant icing
♥
3 tbsp glacé icing
(see p13)
♥
100 g / 3 ½ oz / ½ cup
white cooking chocolate
♥
2 tbsp sprinkles

1 Breadcrumb the flour
and butter, add the sugar
and mix.

2 Shape the mixture into a
ball and roll out the dough
on a floured surface.

26

"Use different coloured sprinkles to make your starfish shimmer!"

3

Cut out shapes using the cutter and put them on the tray. Bake for 15–18 minutes, leave to harden for 2 minutes, then cool on a wire rack.

4

Roll out the icing and cut out stars for the top of the biscuits.

5

Put a dab of glacé icing on the top of a biscuit and stick the icing star to it.

6

Add some melted white chocolate and decorate with sprinkles.

Swirly slices

Makes 15

You will need

baking tray
(2–3 cm / 1 in deep)

baking paper

scales / measuring cups

measuring spoons

saucepan

ziplock bag

rolling pin

wooden spoon

microwave-safe bowl

spoon

knife

Line the baking tray with baking paper.

110g / 4 oz / ½ cup
unsalted butter

♥

2 tbsp / 25 g / 1 oz
caster sugar

♥

2 tbsp / 30 ml / 1 fl. oz
golden syrup

♥

4 tsp cocoa powder

♥

225 g / 8 oz
digestive biscuits

♥

100 g / 3 ½ oz / ⅔ cup
raisins

♥

225 g / 8 oz / 1 ¼ cups
cooking chocolate
(mix of dark and milk)

♥

100 g / 3 ½ oz / ½ cup
white cooking chocolate

1 Put the butter, sugar, syrup and cocoa in a saucepan and melt over a low heat.

2 Put the biscuits in a ziplock bag and crush into small chunks with a rolling pin.

3 Add the biscuits and raisins to the saucepan and mix together well.

4 Put the mixture into the tray and push it down with the back of a spoon.

5 Melt the chocolate and pour it out so that the mix is completely covered, then drizzle white chocolate over the top. Refrigerate for about 2 hours, then take it out of the tray, place it on a board and cut into squares.

"These are best served cold."

Treasure island

Preheat the oven to 180°C / 160°C fan / gas mark 4 and line the cake tins with baking paper.

Serves 16

You will need

4 round cake tins

baking paper

scales / measuring cups

measuring spoons

large bowl

sieve

whisk

wooden spoon

wire rack

plate

knife

400 g / 14 oz / 3 ½ cups
self-raising flour

♥

8 medium eggs
(lightly beaten)

♥

400 g / 14 oz / 1 ¾ cups
unsalted butter

♥

2 drops
vanilla extract

♥

400 g / 14 oz / 2 cups
caster sugar

♥

2 batches / 800 g / 1 lb 8 oz
butter icing (see p13)

♥

200 g / 7 oz
bag of mixed sweets

1 Sieve the flour into a bowl, add the eggs, butter, vanilla extract and sugar and mix for about 2 minutes until it is creamy.

2 Divide the mixture evenly into the cake tins and bake for 15–20 minutes until golden brown, then cool on a wire rack.

3 Place the first cake on a plate and cover with butter icing. Place the remaining 3 cakes on top of the first, with layers of butter icing between them.

4 Ice the sides and top of the layered cake and decorate it with sweets.

"A fun idea for a birthday cake!"

Cutest cake pops

Line a tray with baking paper and half-fill a glass with sugar.

Makes **12**

You will need

tray
baking paper
glass
scales / measuring cups
measuring spoons
large bowl
wooden spoon
12 lollipop sticks
microwave-safe bowl
spoon

6 cupcakes (see p12)
♥
100 g / 3 ½ oz / ½ cup butter icing (see p13)
♥
400 g / 14 oz / 2 ¼ cups cooking chocolate
♥
2 tbsp sprinkles

1 In a bowl, break up the cupcakes until they look like breadcrumbs, then mix in the butter icing.

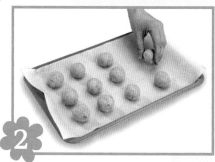

2 Using your hands, squeeze the mixture into 2 cm (1 in) balls, put them on the tray, then freeze for 30 minutes.

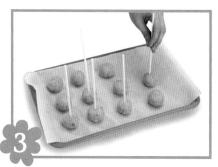

3 Push a lollipop stick into the centre of each cake pop.

4 Melt the chocolate. Take the stick out of each pop, dip the end into the chocolate, then put the stick back in. This will hold it in place.

5 Put the pops in the freezer for another 5 minutes, then dip them into the melted chocolate, making sure they are completely covered.

6 Shake any drips back into the bowl, wait 5 seconds, then dip the pops in the sprinkles. Stand the pops in a glass and cool them in the fridge.

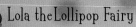

Happy heart pops

Line a tray with baking paper and half-fill a glass with sugar.

Makes 6

You will need

20 x 20 cm (8 x 8 in) baking tray

baking paper

glass

scales / measuring cups

measuring spoons

saucepan

wooden spoon

6 cm (2 ½ in) heart-shaped cookie cutter

6 lollipop sticks

microwave-safe bowl

spoon

---

1 ¾ tbsp / 25 g / 1 oz unsalted butter

♥

200 g / 7 oz / 1 cup white cooking chocolate

♥

125 g / 4 ½ oz / approx. 16 jumbo marshmallows

♥

2 drops pink food colouring

♥

100 g / 3 ½ oz / 4 ⅔ cups toasted rice cereal

♥

2 tbsp sprinkles

1 Melt the butter and half the chocolate in a saucepan over a low heat.

2 Add the marshmallows and food colouring and stir until they have melted.

3 Remove the pan from the heat, add the cereal and stir.

"Perfect for parties and sharing with friends."

4 Spoon the mixture into the tray and spread it with the back of the spoon, then leave it to cool for 10–15 minutes.

5 Cut out heart shapes with the cutter, and then push a stick into the bottom of each heart.

6 Melt the remaining chocolate and drizzle it over the hearts, decorate with sprinkles and stand in the glass.

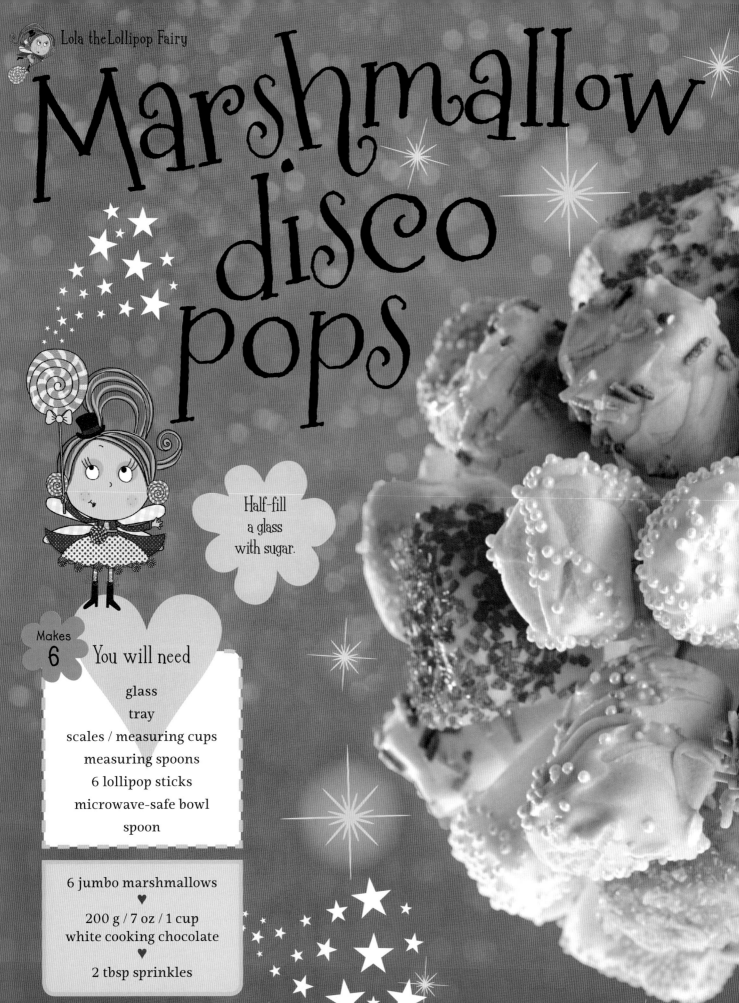

Lola the Lollipop Fairy

Marshmallow disco pops

Half-fill a glass with sugar.

Makes 6

You will need

glass
tray
scales / measuring cups
measuring spoons
6 lollipop sticks
microwave-safe bowl
spoon

6 jumbo marshmallows
♥
200 g / 7 oz / 1 cup
white cooking chocolate
♥
2 tbsp sprinkles

"To make **multi-coloured** disco pops, try adding food colouring to the melted **chocolate**."

1

Put the marshmallows on a tray. Push a lollipop stick into each marshmallow, then freeze for 10 minutes.

2

Melt the chocolate, then dip each marshmallow so it is completely covered.

3

Wait for 5 seconds, then dip the pop in the sprinkles and stand it in the glass to dry.

4

For an edible disco ball, stick the marshmallows on cocktail sticks, then push them into a polystyrene ball.

Lola the Lollipop Fairy

Cookie pops

Half-fill
6 glasses
with sugar,
sprinkles
or sweets.

Makes
6

You will need

6 glasses
tray
scales / measuring cups
measuring spoons
6 lollipop sticks
microwave-safe bowl
spoon

6 cream-centred cookies
♥
200 g / 7 oz / 1 cup
white, plain or milk
cooking chocolate
♥
2 tbsp sprinkles

1

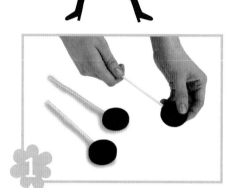

Put the cookies on a tray.
Push a lollipop stick into
the cream centre of each
cookie, then freeze for
5 minutes.

2

Melt the chocolate, then
take the cookies from the
freezer and dip them into
the chocolate until they
are completely covered.

3

Shake any drips back into
the bowl, wait for 5 seconds,
then dip the pops into
the sprinkles.

38

"Try standing the lollipops in glass jars filled with sprinkles."

39

Banutty wands

Half-fill
6 glasses
with sugar
or sweets.

Makes
6

You will need

6 glasses
scales / measuring cups
chopping board
knife
6 wooden lollipop sticks
microwave-safe bowl
spoon
tray / bowl

3 small bananas
♥
175 g / 6 oz / 1 cup
smooth peanut butter
♥
50 g / 1 ¾ oz / 2 ⅓ cups
lightly crushed
puffed-wheat cereal

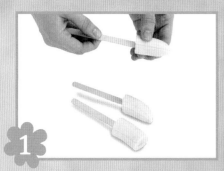

1

Peel and cut the bananas into chunks about 5 cm (2 in) long. Push a stick into the bottom of each chunk.

2

Put the peanut butter in a bowl and microwave for 10–15 seconds, so it is melted but not too runny, and stir. Dip the wands in the bowl so they are completely covered.

3

Put the crushed cereal on a tray or in a bowl and roll the bananas in it, before standing the wands in the glasses.

"Display your wands in jars or even cute flowerpots!"

Magic melts

Makes 6

You will need

2 baking trays
baking paper
scales / measuring cups
measuring spoons
large bowl
hand whisk
3 small bowls
spoon
piping bag
+ 1.25 cm (½ in) tip

3 large eggs
♥
¼ tsp salt
♥
175 g / 6 oz / 1 cup
caster sugar
♥
2–3 drops
different food colourings

1

Separate the eggs and discard the yolks. Add the salt to the egg white and whisk until stiff. Then add the sugar, 1 tablespoon at a time, while mixing.

2

When the mixture is stiff and glossy, separate it into 3 small bowls. Add different food colouring to each bowl and stir.

3

Fill the piping bag and pipe out shapes, rinsing the bag between each colour, or simply spoon the mix onto the tray. Bake for 45–50 minutes, swapping the trays around after 25 minutes.

4

When the meringues are crisp on top, turn off the oven. Open the door slightly and leave the meringues inside for an hour.

5

When the meringues are cold, make them into sandwiches using butter icing, frozen yoghurt or ice cream.

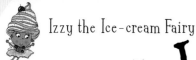

Cool carnival cake

Line the tin with cling film so the film overlaps the edges.

Serves
8

You will need

loaf tin

cling film

scales / measuring cups

measuring spoons

large bowl

electric hand whisk

spoon

medium bowl

microwave-safe bowl

---

16 sponge fingers

♥

250 ml / ½ pint / 1 cup
sweetened condensed milk

♥

200 ml / 7 fl. oz / ¾ cup
double cream

♥

½ tsp vanilla extract

♥

150 ml / ¼ pint / ⅔ cup milk

♥

2 drops
pink food colouring

♥

35 g / 1 ¼ oz / ¼ cup
mashed strawberries

♥

50 g / 1 ¾ oz / ¼ cup
white cooking chocolate

♥

2 tbsp pink sprinkles

1 Place 8 sponge fingers in the tin at intervals so they stand up around the side, then leave to one side.

2 In a large bowl, whisk the condensed milk, cream and vanilla extract until the mixture is quite stiff.

3 Slowly add the milk and continue whisking until it is very stiff, then spoon half the mix into the loaf tin.

4 Mix the food colouring and strawberries into the other half of the mix and spoon it on top of the white mix.

5 Lay the rest of the sponge fingers along the top. Freeze for 4 hours or until the cream is completely frozen.

6 Turn the tin upside-down onto a plate and remove the tin and cling film. Drizzle melted white chocolate over the top.

"Decorate your cake with **pink** sprinkles!"

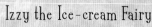
Snow Cookies

Preheat the oven to 200℃ / 180℃ fan / gas mark 6 and line a baking tray with baking paper.

Makes 24

You will need

baking tray
baking paper
scales / measuring cups
measuring spoons
large bowl
wooden spoon
sieve
wire rack

125 g / 4 ½ oz / ½ cup
unsalted butter
♥
100 g / 3 ½ oz / ½ cup
light brown sugar
♥
1 medium egg
(lightly beaten)
♥
1 ½ tsp
vanilla extract
♥
250 g / 8 ¾ oz / 2 ¼ cups
self-raising flour
♥
¼ tsp salt
♥
200 g / 7 oz / 1 cup
white chocolate chips
♥
1 tbsp
icing sugar

1 Put the butter and sugar in a large bowl and mix, then add the egg and vanilla extract.

2 Sieve the flour and salt, add the chocolate chips and mix.

3 Roll the dough into 2 cm (¾ in) balls. Put the balls onto the tray, flatten them with your palm and make sure they are spaced out.

"Bake for 12-15 minutes until golden."

"Cool the cookies on a wire rack, then dust them with icing sugar."

"These cookies are delicious with your favourite milkshake."

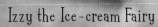
Izzy the Ice-cream Fairy

Coconut ice bites

Line a baking tray with foil.

Makes 16

You will need

20 x 20 cm (8 x 8 in) baking tray

tin foil

scales / measuring cups

sieve

large bowl

wooden spoon

2 medium bowls

spoon

chopping board

knife

250 g / 8 ¾ oz / 2 cups icing sugar

♥

200 ml / 7 fl. oz / 1 cup sweetened condensed milk

♥

250 g / 8 ¾ oz / 3 ⅓ cups desiccated coconut

♥

4–6 drops pink food colouring

" Ask an adult to help you stir as the mixture will be very stiff. "

1 Sieve a spoonful of icing sugar onto the foiled tray.

2 Sieve the rest of the icing sugar into a bowl. Add the milk and coconut then beat together.

48

"Put the tray in the **fridge** for **3** hours. When it is **firm**, turn it out onto a board, remove the foil and cut into **squares**."

3 Divide the mixture into 2 bowls. Add food colouring to one bowl and mix well.

4 Spoon the pink mix into the tray and spread it evenly. Then spoon the white coconut mix on top and smooth flat.

Gingerbread wands

Preheat the oven to 180°C / 160°C fan / gas mark 4 and line a baking tray with baking paper.

Makes 6

You will need

baking tray
baking paper
scales / measuring cups
measuring spoons
large bowl
wooden spoon
sieve
teaspoon
rolling pin
star-shaped cookie cutter
6 lollipop sticks

50 g / 1 ¾ oz / ¼ cup
unsalted butter
♥
2 tbsp / 25 g / 1 oz
brown sugar
♥
3 ½ tbsp / 50 ml / 1 ¾ fl. oz
golden syrup
♥
½ tsp bicarbonate of soda
♥
100 g / 3 ½ oz / 1 cup
plain flour
♥
1 tsp ground ginger
♥
1 tsp cinnamon
♥
½ tsp ground nutmeg
♥
2 tbsp glacé icing
♥
2 tbsp sprinkles

1 In a large bowl, mix the butter and sugar, then add the syrup.

2 Sieve the bicarbonate of soda and flour, add the ginger, cinnamon and nutmeg, and mix.

3 Form a ball with the dough and then roll out.

4 Cut out star shapes and place them on the tray.

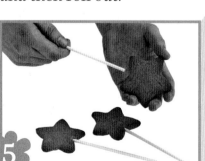

5 Bake for 10–12 minutes until golden brown. As soon as they come out of the oven, push a lollipop stick into each star to make a wand.

"Decorate with your choice of **icing** and **sprinkles**."

50

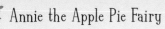

Annie the Apple Pie Fairy

Apple puffs

Preheat the oven to
200°C / 180°C fan /
gas mark 6 and line
a baking tray with
baking paper.

Makes 10

You will need

baking tray

baking paper

scales / measuring cups

measuring spoons

rolling pin

10 cm (4 in)
round cookie cutter

medium bowl

wooden spoon

teaspoon

pastry brush

fork

knife

wire rack

---

1 tbsp plain flour

♥

350 g / 12 ⅓ oz
ready-made puff pastry

♥

100 g / 3 ½ oz / ⅔ cup
mashed blackberries

♥

1 large eating apple,
finely chopped

♥

50 g / 1 ¾ oz / ¼ cup
caster sugar

♥

1 tbsp water

♥

1 tbsp milk

Sprinkle a surface with flour,
roll the pastry, then cut out
10 circles with the cutter.

Mix the blackberries, apple
and half the sugar.

Put 1 teaspoon of the mix on
one side of each circle, then
brush around the edge of
the pastry with water.

Now fold each pastry circle
in half so they look like
half-moons and press the
edges down with a fork.

Brush the top of the moons
with a little milk and
sprinkle sugar on top. Using
a knife, cut a cross shape in
the top of the pastry.

"Bake the puffs for
20-30 minutes
until golden brown,
then cool them on
a wire rack."

52

"Serve the puffs hot with ice cream."

Apple snackles

Makes 8

You will need

10 x 15 cm (4 x 6 in) baking tray

baking paper

scales / measuring cups

measuring spoons

saucepan

wooden spoon

wire rack

---

75 g / 2 ⅔ oz / ⅓ cup unsalted butter

♥

125 g / 4 ½ oz / ⅔ cup caster sugar

♥

85 ml / 3 fl. oz / ⅓ cup golden syrup

♥

225 g / 8 oz / 2 ¾ cups oats

♥

100 g / 3 ½ oz / ⅔ cup raisins

♥

2 small apples, finely chopped

Preheat the oven to 190°C / 170°C fan / gas mark 5 and line a baking tray with baking paper.

1 Melt the butter, sugar and syrup in a pan over a low heat, stirring gently.

2 Take the pan off the heat and stir in the oats, raisins and chopped apple.

3 Spoon the mixture into the tray and press down with the back of a spoon. Bake for 15–20 minutes until golden brown.

"Cool on a wire rack, then cut into cute slices."

Annie the Apple Pie Fairy

chocey apples

Line a tray with baking paper.

1 Push a lollipop stick into each apple.

2 Melt the chocolate, then dip the apple into the chocolate and make sure it is completely covered.

3 Shake any drips back into the bowl, wait 5 seconds, then dip the coated apple into the sprinkles, nuts or marshmallows and leave on the tray to dry.

Makes **6**

You will need

tray
baking paper
scales / measuring cups
6 lollipop sticks
microwave-safe bowl
spoon

6 small sweet apples, washed
♥
400 g / 14 oz / 2 ¼ cups milk, white or dark cooking chocolate
♥
100 g / 3 ½ oz sprinkles, nuts or mini marshmallows

Cutie pies

Makes
12

You will need

cupcake tray

scales / measuring cups

measuring spoons

rolling pin

8 cm (3 in) fluted
cookie cutter

small heart-shaped
cookie cutter

pastry brush

medium bowl

teaspoon

wire rack

Preheat the oven to
190°C / 170°C fan /
gas mark 5 and grease
the tray with butter.

1 tbsp unsalted butter
♥
1 tbsp plain flour
♥
350 g / 12 ⅓ oz
ready-made
shortcrust pastry
♥
1 tbsp milk
♥
1 tbsp brown sugar
♥
2 medium-sized eating
apples, finely chopped
♥
2 tbsp / 25 g / ¾ oz
caster sugar
♥
100 g / 3 ½ oz / 1 ¼ cups
muesli

1

Roll the pastry on a floured surface. Cut out 12 circles and put them in the tray.

2

Cut out 12 hearts. Brush them with a little milk and sprinkle them with brown sugar. Then leave to one side.

3

Mix the chopped apples and caster sugar in a bowl.

4

Put a teaspoon of mix in each pastry case and sprinkle with a little muesli, then place a pastry heart on top.

"Bake for 25-30 minutes until golden brown, then cool on a wire rack."

Twinkly treats

Preheat the oven to
190℃ / 170℃ fan /
gas mark 5 and line
a baking tray with
baking paper.

Makes 16

You will need

baking tray

baking paper

scales / measuring cups

measuring spoons

large bowl

sieve

rolling pin

5 cm (2 in)
round cookie cutter

lollipop stick

wire rack

4 cm (1 ½ in)
fluted cookie cutter

knife

ribbon

---

75 g / 2 ⅔ oz / ⅔ cup
plain flour

♥

50 g / 1 ¾ oz / 3 ½ tbsp
unsalted butter

♥

2 tbsp / 25 g / ¾ oz
caster sugar

♥

150 g / 5 ⅓ oz
white fondant icing

♥

2 tbsp glacé icing (see p13)

♥

200 g / 7 oz / 1 cup
sugar-coated chocolates

1 Breadcrumb the flour and butter, add the sugar and mix.

2 Shape into a ball and roll out the dough on a floured surface.

3 Cut out 12 shapes with the round cutter, put them on the tray and bake for 15–18 minutes until golden.

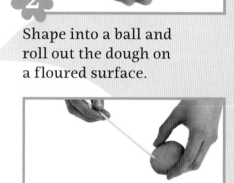

4 As soon as they come out, make a hole in the top of each cookie with a lollipop stick and cool on a wire rack.

5 Roll out the fondant icing and cut out 12 shapes with the fluted cutter.

6 Put a dab of glacé icing on the top of a cookie and stick the fondant icing shape to it.

"Decorate the treats with sugar-coated **chocolates.**"

"Thread ribbon through the holes and hang your treats on a **tree**"

61

Katie the Candy Cane Fairy

Candy cane crunch

Line a baking tray with baking paper.

Makes 12

You will need

baking tray

baking paper

scales / measuring cups

microwave-safe bowl

spoon

ziplock bag

rolling pin

340 g / 12 oz / 2 cups
dark / milk chocolate

♥

8 peppermint
candy canes

♥

340 g / 12 oz / 2 cups
white chocolate

2 Put the candy canes into the bag, seal it, then use a rolling pin to roll or smash the canes into small pieces.

3 Melt the white chocolate, then stir in ¾ of the candy cane pieces. Pour the melted white chocolate mix into the tray.

1 Melt the dark chocolate, then pour it into the tray and spread it evenly. Place the tray in the fridge until the chocolate has set.

4 Sprinkle the rest of the candy canes on top and smooth down with a spoon. Place the tray in the fridge until hard.

62

Index

Copyright © 2013

make believe ideas ltd

The Wilderness, Berkhamsted, Hertfordshire, HP4 2AZ.

All rights reserved. No part of this publication may be reproduced, stored in a retrieval system, or transmitted in any form or by any means, electronic, mechanical, photocopying, recording, or otherwise, without the prior written permission of the copyright owner.

www.makebelieveideas.com

Concept: Joanna Bicknell
Recipes: Angela Weekes, LoveMyCake.com
Food photographer: Andy Snaith
Food stylists: Joanna Bicknell and Annie Simpson
Recipe testing: Julie Howell and
Jane Manning of the Make Believe Café
Illustrations: Lara Ede
Designer: Mark Richards
Editor: Fiona Boon

Weight

Metric	Imperial	Metric	Imperial
10 g	⅓ oz	170 g	6 oz
15 g	½ oz	200 g	7 oz
20 g	¾ oz	225 g	8 oz
30 g	1 oz	255 g	9 oz
45 g	1 ½ oz	285 g	10 oz
50 g	1 ¾ oz	340 g	12 oz
60 g	2 oz	400 g	14 oz
70 g	2 ½ oz	450 g	1 lb
85 g	3 oz	500 g	1 lb 2 oz
100 g	3 ½ oz	600 g	1 lb 5 oz
115 g	4 oz	700 g	1 lb 9 oz
130 g	4 ½ oz	800 g	1 lb 12 oz
140 g	5 oz	900 g	2 lb
155 g	5 ½ oz	1 kg	2 lb 3 oz

Oven temperatures

Celsius	Fahrenheit	Gas mark
140°C	275°F	1
150°C	300°F	2
160°C	325°F	3
180°C	350°F	4
190°C	375°F	5
200°C	400°F	6
220°C	425°F	7
230°C	450°F	8
240°C	475°F	9

If you have a fan-assisted oven, reduce the temperature by at least 20 degrees.